LIGHT UP YOUR SOUL

10 Powerful Ways to Create a More Fulfilling Life

Sally Scofield

You must make a choice
to take a chance or
your life will never change.

-UNKNOWN

DEDICATION

I would like to dedicate this book to my aunt Ella. You inspire me to help make this world a better and better place...in my own way!

RAVING REVIEWS

"Exactly What You'll Need!"

"Sally Scofield does a fantastic job anticipating exactly what you'll need to *Light Up Your Soul*. Her page-turning book is packed with practical advice on how to *Create a More Fulfilling Life*. This was a clearly thought out product made with love, and I could feel Scofield supporting me every step of the way." --Lena Anani, Author of *OMG Do It Now: Be the Voice You Want to Hear in the World*

"I Would Highly Recommend This Book!"

"Sally Scofield's words are positive, uplifting, and will definitely *Light Up Your Soul*! Scofield's *10 Positive Ways to Create a More Fulfilling Life* are truly inspiring and provides a clear understanding through her examples and techniques on how to live a joyful and enjoyable life. I would highly recommend this book to anyone that wants to gain a positive outlook on life and create the life that brings them happiness." -- Crystal Simpelo, Author of *The Colorful Expressions of Your Soul: A Mandala Coloring Book and Meditative Creative Journal,* CrystalSimpelo.com

"Healthy And Refreshing Solutions!"

"Sally relates to us with real life problems and demonstrates how to change these issues into healthy and refreshing solutions. She shares her struggles on negative thinking and shows us how to transform our thoughts into a fresh positive perspective. If you are looking for some motivation to become happier and feel balanced with life, *Light Up Your Soul* is the book for you!" -- Katie Van Eynde, Author of *Motivate Your Magnetic Mind: 10 Simple Ways to Attract Positive Vibes In All Areas of Your Life*, KatieLovesLife.com

"Lighthearted And Joyful!"

"Thank you Sally Scofield, for a practical guide to shifting our thinking and our being. The subject of introspective work has been given a lighthearted and joyful facelift, and it will make people WANT to roll up their sleeves and get busy transforming their lives. This book is a great addition to the 'constantly used' section of anyone's library." --Marie Denkinger, Hand Analyst & Sage CEO, Life Purpose Wisdom, LifePurposeWisdom.com

"Turn Your Life Towards Happiness Today!"

"This treasure chest of practical and powerful ways to turn your life toward happiness today is brought to you by the ray of sunshine named Sally Scofield. Her love and compassion for you the reader sings through these pages. You will get to know her as I know her and be inspired to step into your best life." --Mercy Burton Russell, MSW, Relationship Systems Specialist

"Real Tools For Real People!"

"Real tools for real people from an author who walks her talk and speaks from her heart. Simple steps with the power for deep transformation--Sally Scofield teaches you how to give wings to your soul!" --Lindy MacLaine, theCurseoftheNeverland.com, Author

"Shares From Her Heart!"

"Reading Sally Scofield's book is like listening to a trusted, wise, and loving friend who shares from her heart and real experience what 'really works' if you want to live a happy life." --Elizabeth Haines, Life Coach, RenegadeRetirement.com

"Simple, Practical, and Playful!"

"*Light Up Your Soul* is an insightful, delightful book! Sally Scofield has a gift for sharing profound wisdom in a simple, practical and playful way. I especially love the way she weaves personal stories throughout, engaging the reader in feeling 'if she can do it, so can I!' In essence, the entire book is a beautiful blueprint for life transformation!" --Evie Kane, Licensed Psychotherapist-Shaman-Spiritual Coach, South Pasadena, CA

"An Easy To Use Guide!"

"Sally Scofield has gifted the world with her light and knowledge through *Light Up Your Soul*. As an easy to use guide it is a banquet to chose from. Meditation? Journaling? Exercising and Gratitude? No problem…she covers these and more in a book you will use over and over, and probably want to gift to family and friends too." --Marjorie Schoelles, Corporate VP and Author/Illustrator, *Now I Wish Upon A Pearl*, MermaidSand.com

CONTENTS

ACKNOWLEDGEMENTS

I would like to acknowledge the following people that have helped me on the path of writing this book:

Mom and Dad for the best possible upbringing,

Mike Schafer for his unwavering love and support,

Baeth Davis, Pamelah Landers and Lee Milteer for planting the seed,

Lena Anani for being nothing short of amazing in this whole process,

To my most diverse network of friends and family who have been there for me throughout the years and believe in me,

And to the open-minded people in this world that know we can make it a better place by starting with ourselves,

I'm so grateful to all of YOU!

INTRODUCTION

"Tell me, what is it you plan to do
with your one wild and precious life."
- Mary Oliver

Have you ever felt even the slightest hint that there may be something else out there for you, whether it is more joy, peace, abundance, or simplicity that you could have? I want you to know that it is in your power to create what it is that you want.

It's amazing how we have turned into such creatures of habit in our daily lives that we become stuck in our routine. We grow blinders to possibilities and start to unknowingly overlook ways of becoming "unstuck" in our problems. I came to realize that I was becoming surrounded more and more by people that were complaining about the same things, and I was turning into one of them. My health issues, my job, my relationships, and my money felt less and less fulfilling. I was falling into a rut and was starting to feel like I could not do anything about it. Then something in me clicked. I knew there had to be more to life than what I was living.

In opening my mind, I started to see more and more possibilities of what is out there that I can accomplish. Every dream of mine is coming true. If I were still on the complaining train, I would not have noticed all of the wonderful, though somewhat untraditional, opportunities that I have taken. If I had second-guessed or dismissed the goals and aspirations that came to me then I would still be in that safe, secure place that I was at in my past, but I was not fulfilled in that place. So while I will never judge anybody who decides to dismiss those little thoughts that come into your head, I just want to dare you to dream. What if you could make one of your dreams come true? What if you could make all of your dreams come true? And the best part is, you do not have to know the details of how to make it all happen now. It is a process, and it develops as you incorporate the chapters of this book into your life. Give your life color instead of living in black and white all of the time.

I love to think back on all of the times that I have dared to go beyond the norm. All of those moments have been defining and have given me a life worth living. It encourages me to keep doing more of the fun things in life that I was meant to do. So whatever kind of life you desire, I am telling you, there are no more excuses not to have it. I can see you waking up in the morning with a smile on your face, excited for the new day and what you have planned for it!

My name is Sally Scofield, and I am writing this book to help you improve the quality of your existence and to help you create your more fulfilling life! Let's light it up! I am super excited about making a positive difference in your life!

I had a burning desire to help people that were in my shoes. I wanted to help people that had a similar sensation that I had that something is missing. I felt guilty, initially, for feeling this way. At first, I felt as if people would look at me for taking everything I had for granted or assume that I was being selfish for wanting more goodness in my life, but the more this feeling kept nagging at me, the more I realized that having a truly fulfilling life is my (and your) divine right! When I discovered these great ways of helping me get to where I wanted to be, I knew I wanted to share it with as many people as possible. And what better way than writing a book to get started?

I am living breathing proof that the topics in this book are valid ways to acquire the life that is desired. I have done tremendous amounts of research to test the ways that do work. In a sense, I did the trial and error process myself to get you to the good stuff, because the last thing I wanted to do was waste anybody's time.

I like to keep things short, sweet, and to the point. You will find this book a quick and easy read! The most important part is that you use what you learn in this book, and weave it into your life.

My intention is to pass on all of the good things that I have come across, because I believe that sharing these 'not-so-traditional' ways will make great breakthroughs for you as well! I am so happy, grateful and proud of you for taking the steps to get what it is that you can have!

JOURNALING

Writing things down has a tremendous impact. It's funny; I did not realize at first what amazing things can come from journaling. A lot of the time, my getting results all boiled down to my journaling. It still seems somewhat surreal to me! What better time, than to start right now to journal, and start receiving the benefits of it!

Start now, just write your thoughts down. Simple, right? Do this daily. As you go through each of these chapters, journal what comes up for you. For example, in the next chapter, be sure to write and especially narrow down your values. Writing things down shows intention, and there is nothing like a clear intention to get the ball rolling! This opens the universe up into having a clear "GO" sign to giving you what you want! In each chapter, remember to incorporate journaling with each activity.

When I started to journal, I began to see a shift. It was not an "all in a day" kind of thing. It was subtle, but a great subtle! And it's funny, because it is one of those things that sometimes I have to remind myself to do when I feel like I need improvement in an area of my life! I notice a difference even if I have missed just a couple of days. When I started to journal, it was initially just jotting down my core values, because I wanted to get back to basics to find my purpose in life and to get more fulfillment. Then, I narrowed those down, which helped me gain clarity about what I really wanted and more importantly why I wanted it and how having it would serve me. It weeded out a lot of clutter in what I actually wanted in life.

I went on to write about experiences I wanted. I then took it a step further and wrote as if I had those experiences in that very moment, with all of the details included (using all five senses), feeling grateful as if it was in my life then and there. Not long after that, I began to be surprised at how the little and big things began to pop up; I kid you not, those things I had wanted and journaled about began to happen. This led me to have a separate journal I call my "Evidence Journal." This is a super fun one, because I write about how these things actually came into my life and the fun, surprising ways in which they happened! If I even think about having a dull moment, I look upon this journal and I "re-realize" what the power of journaling can do!

I know this woman, Beth, whose husband tragically passed away. She was having a very hard time with it and seemed to lose herself as the days passed. She could not get back into the swing of life, until she started to journal. She wrote her heart out daily. Slowly but surely her life began to have light in it again. She made an amazing comeback and now is very successful doing that for a living, helping others that need that 'fix' in their lives.

As you keep a journal and write at least a little bit each day, you will most likely start to see how things are changing for the better. Releasing fears and feelings that come up can help clear them. Writing down things you want to have and accomplish may suddenly start to happen. It is so fun looking back and saying, "See! I manifested this!" and then writing it down as evidence. What you drew into your life can accelerate the act of bringing more things that you want into your life.

Also, just writing something down, whether it is a problem or something you want to experience, the act of writing it down on paper and looking at it from that point of view, is a totally different perspective. Sometimes a problem may seem smaller or more insignificant, easier to solve. In breaking down ways to achieve a goal, if you write out the small steps that you may have to take, it makes it seem easier to obtain, all by writing it down. I encourage you to try it and see what happens!

So now you see how writing things down can show intention, assist in giving clarity, help you move through things and also manifest things along the way. In this next chapter, you will see how to use your journaling skills to define your core values, and how this aids in getting more clarity, more ease in decision making, and realizing what it is that you really want!

I cannot wait to see the way journaling will change your life for the positive, as it has for so many.

DEFINE YOUR VALUES

"Your habits become your values,

your values become your destiny."

- Mahatma Gandhi

Getting back to basics on what you REALLY want (and why you want it) provides so much clarity.

When you sit down and get back to the basics of what you want, gaining that clarity, it makes it so much easier to define what it is you really want and why you want it. In uncovering your top values, making decisions gets easier, your goals become clearer, and any sense of being overwhelmed melts away. Your ego gets put to the side, and you can focus on what is important. If you want to simplify things, this is your ticket! Defining this information right now will make things so much clearer!

From the list of values below choose about twenty items that you feel best represent what is most important to you and what you want out of life. Feel free to add in your own words, this is just an idea to get your mind going.

Abundance	Compassion	Education
Acceptance	Competence	Efficiency
Acknowledgement	Concentration	Elegance
Adventure	Confidence	Empathy
Agility	Consciousness	Endurance
Appreciation	Contribution	Excellence
Assertiveness	Control	Expressive
Awareness	Cooperation	Faith
Balance	Courage	Family
Beauty	Creativity	Focus
Belonging	Dependability	Forgiveness
Bliss	Desire	Freedom
Brilliance	Difference	Fulfillment
Calm	Discovery	Fun
Change	Diversity	Generosity
Charity	Divinity	Giving
Cleanliness	Duty	Goodness
Community	Ease	Gratitude
Growth	Modesty	Respect
Happiness	Money	Responsibility

Harmony	Motivation	Romance
Health	Nature	Safety
Honesty	Nonviolence	Security
Hope	Nurturing	Self-esteem
Humility	Openness	Selflessness
Humor	Optimism	Serenity
Improvement	Organization	Service
Independence	Originality	Simplicity
Innovation	Passion	Spirit
Integrity	Peace	Spirituality
Intelligence	Perseverance	Stability
Intuition	Persistence	Status
Joy	Pleasure	Strength
Kindness	Positivity	Style
Leadership	Power	Success
Liberty	Practicality	Timeliness
Logic	Proactive	Tradition
Love	Quality	Travel
Loyalty	Radiance	Truth
Luxury	Reason	Variety
Making	Relationships	Wealth
Maturity	Religion	Well-being
Meaning	Resourcefulness	Wisdom

Now take your twenty and narrow it down to twelve, then down to six, and eventually choose your Top Three Values. For me, it was easier to narrow them down by sub-categorizing obvious ones. For example, Joy, Happiness, Bliss, Harmony and Peace all came under Well-being for me. Then I ended up funneling that into the Health Category, which is ultimately one of my Top Three, because in having my great health, I am able to enjoy all things so much more! Without it, my life would not be as fabulous!

Now that you have your Top Three, find somewhere to post them so they will always be in sight and they can inspire you constantly. Keep them on the fridge, by your desk, or have it be on your bed stand so it's the first thing you see in the morning and the last thing you think about at the end of the day. Your daily choices will start to reflect them; it's great!

When I actually sat my butt down to do this, I had to laugh. The things I ended up picking for my Top Three were not what I initially would have thought. It was an interesting realization, and that is why it is so important to do this exercise; it is a learning experience! When I focused on my Top Ten, I considered these more in my daily decision-making and I in turn began to actually make wiser decisions! It seems like such a simple thing, like we should just "know," but it is amazing to see the daily moves that we make mindlessly. Also after sitting down and doing this exercise myself, I realized how my Top Three values could possibly change throughout my life. There are landmarks and experiences in one's life that may alter their values. So I think it is important to 'check in' and do this exercise every so often to make sure you are staying on track!

My friend Eddie was the sole provider for his wife, Heidi, and their three kids. Heidi had always enjoyed working, but things had changed after she had the three kids. After discussing it, they decided she would stay home and take care of the kids, and Eddie would work overtime if they needed extra money. It was nice to have that extra money, but with that came the stress of not spending that time with the ones he truly loved. Feeling like a hamster on a wheel, he would come home, great paycheck in hand, but be so exhausted that he would go to bed and have to get up early to do it all over again. He felt he was becoming more irritated and wondered if there was a better way. One morning as he was leaving the house to go to work, he saw a magazine article relating to solving the problem that he was having. Inside, it had the exercise to find your Top Three core values and showed how things in your life would start to go in the direction that you wanted if you just incorporated making decisions using them. So on the train to work he figured out his Top Three.

His were family, happiness and abundance. He made the excuse that he was working so hard for his family, but realized in an instant that all they wanted was to spend time with him. He did not want to be the person that within the blink of an eye missed his kid's childhoods. That very night, after a much-needed talk with Heidi, they decided he would take a job that came up at a more local office for the company he worked for. She explained to him that she did not want to hurt his feelings in any way or make him feel like he was not providing enough, but she wanted to go back to work part-time during school hours. This gave them more abundance of family time, their income ended up being more than before, and they were all happier to spend more quality time together.

After implementing this, it is amazing the clarity and simplicity in decision-making that can happen. Do you know off the cuff what your core values are? Won't it be neat to see if you have been working inline with your decisions as of this date? Do you think you will be surprised? I laugh when I think about my experience in doing the exercise! But I am so glad that I did!

Now that you have more clarity through defining your core values, and you understand better how this aids in getting more ease in decision-making and realizing what it is that you really want, we will look at some things that may be holding you back that you do not even realize. We will look at your self-limiting beliefs and how to become aware of them, how to make moves to overcome them and reset your brain into getting you the life that you want and deserve.

Now that you have your core values in mind, do you not feel the clarity and instant simplicity that it brings into your life?

SELF-LIMITING BELIEFS

"Use 'why?' to help you follow
the breadcrumbs back to the problem."
- Stephen Richards

You will be amazed at how your subconscious runs the thoughts that you have every day. With it being known that 90% of your brain capabilities are run with subconscious thoughts, this definitely affects your decision process. The other 10% is the conscious brain. The majority of these thoughts were actually formed at a very young age, and you probably do not realize what power they have.

What better time than now to take control of more of your thoughts and use them in a good way! Uncover the things that you don't realize are holding you back and become the best person that you can be. If you could improve in every way, wouldn't you want to know how? It's a no-brainer to me!

First, you need to write one goal of yours. It can be anything at all. Once you have written it down, make two columns on your paper, splitting the paper in half down the middle, making a left and right column. On the left side, write all of the reasons why you can and will accomplish this goal. As you do this, you will most likely have thoughts that come up that are reasons that you cannot or do not think you can accomplish this goal. Those are put into the right hand column. Write down everything that comes up for you.

You may notice some of these common examples:

"I could never reach this goal realistically"

"I do not have enough/the right education to do this"

"Money is the root of all evil"

"I do not deserve this kind of life that I want"

"It is too hard to maintain this life, even if I were to get it"

"No matter what I do, I can never seem to get ahead in life"

"I need money in order to make money"

"I do not have the time to do what I want to do"

"Big thighs run in my family, so why will I be any different?"

"My family/friends would not approve of this"

"It's going to be so hard to do this."

These are just the tip of the iceberg of some of the things that you may discover upon this activity. Do not write anything off that comes up or push them to the side if they seem silly; it is those that could be the bugaboos that are holding you back. You are most likely going to have to make a change in the way you think, to accomplish this goal that you have. Let that thought sink in.

Now that you have uncovered some of them, what will it take for you to overcome them? This may be different for each individual. I started by noticing these thoughts as they came up. When I started looking into writing this book, boy did my self-limiting beliefs come up. "Who do you think you are? Why do you think you are qualified? Don't you think you're getting a little too big for your britches? It takes forever to write a book! Who will buy this book of yours? You are really putting yourself out there for people to criticize now! Maybe you should just play small and stay safe?" Wow, I had a lot of mean things to say to myself! I looked at the left side of my list, the reasons why and it totally outweighed the right side. So from there, I knew I needed to work through the self-limiting beliefs! Warning: These little buggers came up time and time again for me. I wish I could tell you that they just went away, as I became aware of them, but I cannot. It did help knowing what they were, so I could set those thoughts aside as I was doing my thing. I would notice them and say, "Thanks 'Ego' for looking out for me, but I believe I am onto something better here", and I would drive on.

I then stumbled upon Tapping, otherwise known as EFT (Emotional Freedom Technique) for my most stubborn and unwavering self-limiting beliefs. It is a proven method of helping the cortisol levels in your body, showing measurable effects on a body's nervous system. This process sounded crazy to me, but I knew that if I wanted to get beyond it, I had to do something I had never done before. All of the scientific information was great to know, but I just wanted something to get over this "useless" baggage I was carrying around, so I started to tap on my acupressure points to release my old beliefs and replace them with my awesome new beliefs.

To get you started, the next few paragraphs will provide you with a crash course in tapping. If you are a visual learner, then be sure to visit www.SallyScofield.com/EFT to watch my training video on how to "tap" effectively.

Your tapping points will be your karate chop point on one of your hands, your inside eyebrow point, the outside of your eye point, under the eye point, under the nose point, hollow of the chin point, collarbone point, under the arm point and the top of your head point. Keep a mental note to do it in this order.

First I write down a goal. I use a scale of 1-10 of how strong I feel this is impossible at the time, with 1 being totally possible and 10 being totally impossible, no way, no how.

I use my right hand to tap with because I am right handed. I take my glasses off if I am wearing them, to access my points easier. I tap the left points of my body because it is easier for me. I will give an example of exactly how I do it, because it was easiest for me to see how someone else did it first. I follow the same basic guide each time, but different things come up for me with different scenarios, so you should be flexible and flow according to your own situation.

So I have written down my goal and given it a solid score of 9.

Taking two fingers from my right hand, I gently tap on my left hand karate chop point and say:

"Even though I want to make a difference in writing a book, it feels impossible. I mean, who do I think I am? It's impossible. I am just going to honor my feelings about this.

Even though I love the thought of this goal, it still feels impossible for me to accomplish. I am just going to honor this right now, even though it sounds negative, I am just going to honor it.

Even though this feels impossible right now, I am very open to shifting this feeling"

(Notice the "Even though" phrase said three times to start while tapping on the karate chop point.)

With the same two fingers, I continue to tap on the remainder of my points, in the order given, and say what comes up for me. No forcing involved. I tap on a point for as long as I say a thought or a couple of sentences and then move to the next point, and then tap on that while saying the next couple of thoughts, and so on.

My thoughts as they come up go something like this, "This really feels impossible for me. Other people have done this before, but why would I think that I could do it?" (next point) "Plus, this would be really hard."(next point) "I'm not really smart enough, nor do I have the resources to do it" (next point) "I would probably get writer's block, like I hear so much about" (next point) "It costs a lot to publish a book, I don't have the money for that" (next point) "It just seems undoable for someone like me" (next point) " It really feels impossible" (next point) "Wow, I am really hard on myself. I would love to change my way of thinking about this." I then take a deep breath, exhaling all of those negative beliefs. I then take a look at my goal that I have written down and write the score of how I feel about it now.

It feels like there is hope and there is a sense of possibility, like maybe, just maybe, I am being too hard on myself. So now, I feel a shift in my own personal score. I give myself a 7. I am doing it. I am subtly shifting! I do this as many times as needed, until I get to at least a 2-3. This can also narrow down your self-limiting beliefs, because you will hone in on that one recurring thought that keeps tripping you up and holding you back. Along the way I have received intuitive hits on how I could make it happen and I write them down immediately!

So now that I am in a better place, I start at the karate chop point again. I say, "I am so glad my goal feels attainable. I do not know all of the details in how I will get there, but I am open to a multitude of different ways that it can happen. This feels so good. Even though I have an inner voice that is being skeptical, I am going to honor that. However, the truth is, there is a ton of different ways that this CAN happen for me and I am going to say yes to all of them!"

Now, tapping on my other points, I say, "How is this going to happen? What if I fail?" (next point) "It is scary, I have to admit, but it is also exciting!" (next point) "I like to think of all of the faces of the people that I will help make a difference in their life" (next point) "I do not have to know exactly how it is going to happen at exactly this moment" (next point) "Life is about fun little surprises and I am going to embrace them as they come" (next point) "I am excited to see how this will come about for me!" (next point) "I have knowledge in what I want to write about, so yes, this does make me qualified!" (next point) "All of my book material has worked for me and other people, and I know that people would like to see my living proof examples, so YES this is more than possible, I just have to do it!"

When I get done, I always feel like a million bucks! It works great for getting out of these ruts that we like to dig ourselves into.

When I realized that the thoughts in my own brain were holding me back, it made perfect sense. I did have to do the exercise to uncover them. Once I knew them, I could start to retrain my brain into thinking healthy, positive thoughts about all situations! This has improved my relationships, my self-confidence, my moneymaking abilities, my health and well being.

After Bill sat down and figured out what was really holding him back, he was in a state of disbelief. "Really?" he said, "I remember hearing that as a kid, money is evil and that only the rich get richer and the poor get poorer". All he knew was that no matter how hard he tried to make ends meet, he just could not get ahead. "But it can't be because of a silly little thought like that!" After pondering it though, he realized that he really did not have anything to lose by trying to overcome this, because changing his subconscious was not going to cost anything. He had originally thought that people would think he was nuts to consider this "woo-woo" idea, but he was so in debt now he did not care as long as it helped him get out of this hole! So he said he had succeeded with the technique of Tapping, also known as EFT (Emotional Freedom Technique).

He would acknowledge his 'old' feelings as they came up, and then do the tapping process on particular acupressure points and affirm his new thought patterns. He immediately felt relief and shortly thereafter he started to see a change. There was a definite shift in his consciousness. He got a promotion at work (later, he found out that a lot of it had to do with the way he started to present himself in a better manner) and things were getting better and better for him.

When you uncover your self-limiting beliefs you will be a little bit dumbfounded. You will most likely be amazed at how these 'little' thoughts can have such an effect on your being. Becoming aware of them all is the majority of the battle that you can overcome. Working through them to overcome them and 'resetting' how you want things to be is the way to move through your life with more ease. I have also uncovered deeper self-limiting beliefs since I have started using this process, ones that were not as obvious at first. Therefore, I would recommend checking in with yourself and doing this exercise often!

Now that you are aware of your self-limiting beliefs and how you can make moves to overcoming them and reset your brain into getting you the life that you want and deserve, we will move into more subconscious thoughts. You will see an explanation of how thoughts of yourself and others can affect you. Included in this is stopping your negative mind chatter and replacing it with good feeling thoughts.

It is essential to replace self-limiting beliefs in order to ascend in life.

BE CONSCIOUS

"Control of consciousness
determines the quality of life."
- Mihaly Csikszentmihalyi

When one has not-so-nice mind chatter, it acts as a poison residing in one's self. As for putting yourself down, you can unknowingly stop yourself from ascending in life. (Perhaps stopping you from trying a new job, a trendy outfit, or adventure). We've all done it. This can ultimately lead to regrets: "I should have taken that trip when I was young." Sound familiar? This in a sense makes us 'wrong' and we end up feeling even worse about ourselves; guilt, regret, and sadness will eventually spiral you downward.

When one puts others down, there is a possibility of hidden jealousy: "Who does she think she is, wearing something that trendy?" Deep down inside you, you may be thinking that you wanted that exact outfit and wished you looked that good in it. This also goes for gossip. Stop any and all gossip right now! I always laugh at how people say they can not stand gossip, then minutes later, they indulge in speaking of the latest rumor and enhance it by giving their take on it.

I dare you to start being more conscious of these thoughts when they come up. When they do, mentally say, "Stopping that thought" and immediately change to a good feeling thought, even if you have to think about a completely different subject! You will start to feel yourself feeling better as you do this! And when someone starts to gossip, stop them in their tracks. Perhaps they do not realize they are doing it. At least let them know you are not comfortable listening to it. And if you are not comfortable with doing that, you can always change the subject. Stick to it!

Being conscious of this will start to change you into being a more positive person. Unless of course, you want to go around thinking crappy thoughts, which will in turn bring crappy things to you. I prefer all good!

Start now by just noticing your thoughts as they come up. Wherever you are, whatever you are doing throughout the day, take mental note. As someone is confiding in you, are you distracted by what they are wearing? Are you distracted by whatever else is going on in the room? Are you thinking that what they are saying seems wrong? Are you criticizing yourself for saying something "stupid"?

If you are noticing negative mind chatter coming up, set it aside and consciously change that thought for a better one. Instead of thinking, "Why do I think I can accomplish that?", turn that thought into, "Wow, look at all of the great things in my life I have accomplished as of now! I am certainly capable of doing this!" The more that you notice your thoughts and alter them for the better, you will notice your life will start to change in a good way! I am excited for you as I write this!

I encourage you to be conscious about what you say to and about yourself. Your subconscious cannot decipher jokes or literal statements. When you say, "I'm so fat". Your subconscious engages your body to give you EXACTLY what you say. Even if you despise yourself so much, start by saying, "I am getting healthier and healthier every day in every way". Reach for better feeling thoughts. When you think these good thoughts often, you will see the changes happening. It is such a rewarding process!

Notice the theme of what you write in your daily journal. Go back and read what you have written in the past and see if you notice a theme. Negative? Optimistic? While I used to think it was a good idea to vent in my journal, I learned that I had to change my thinking pattern to being more positive. An optimistic tone was necessary, so I would not spiral downward into my not so great place. I began to notice that my positive thoughts were attracting more good things in my life; therefore, I began to choose to consciously think and write good things in order to get more of the same. Try it!

It shocked me when I started to realize that for the naturally positive person that I am, I still had some crummy thoughts that liked to lurk around in my mind! I still catch myself thinking a 'not-so-nice' thought and mentally say, "You know, that's not like me to think that way!" And then I re-route to a better feeling thought! It has really changed my perception of things. I feel wiser in general and more compassionate towards others now. I feel better about myself, and others as well.

My friend Ron and I were talking one day about things that would be fun to have. He had always wanted to get a sports car. He made good money and it seemed like an easy thing for him to achieve in my eyes. I asked him why he had never bought one. He threw out the old, "What makes you think I'm so special to deserve that?" If I had not been sitting, I would have fallen down. "Seriously?" I said, "Who have you been talking to? Of course you deserve it!" Then I proceeded to tell him all of the reasons as I saw, from an outsider looking in, of why he should get one.

He did not disagree with all of the reasons, but he was hung up on the deserving part of it. When we talked more about why he felt that way, I found the culprit. His self-worth issues were getting the best of him. Upon further discussions, after we uncovered this bugaboo of his, he decided to play the "What If" game. He began to get excited thinking more and more about it. He finally decided that he would entertain the thought of owning one and started to look through the car ads.

A few months later, he found a smoking deal on a car like he had described to me. He told me later that when the thought came up in his head about him not deserving it, he set it to the side and wisely went about the deal. He admits it is one of the best things he has ever done! He knows that if he had kept thinking that he did not deserve it, he would have always held some regret, and he is able to truly enjoy owning his sports car now.

In another example, Marie was a hardworking single mom, and worked at a local supermarket on most weekdays and a gas station not far from her house on her days off from that. She did not have a lot of spare time to spend with her 2 girls, who were in grade school at the time. Marie is one of those creative people that could turn a dog dish into a beautiful lampshade. She has the creative eye that can turn garbage into gold.

On her time off, she would repurpose items. Her girls would enjoy helping her, and they were able to spend time together. She had all of these things throughout her home and would give items away for birthday presents or Christmas gifts. I was lucky enough to receive one of these items and I remember exclaiming, "Marie, where did you get this? This is so awesome, I've never seen anything like it before!"

She nonchalantly told me it was something she and the girls had put together, and pawned off the compliment. "It's nothing big, just something we did in our spare time". The item she gave me was one of those things that not only was I a fan of, but other people that came over to my house would ogle over. I knew then and there, I was not biased, and that she had a potential business on her hands! In talking with her about this, she explained all of the reasons why she could not and should not do it. I suggested, "So what is it going to hurt if you just try to sell a couple of your items in the store downtown that promotes locally made items?" She finally decided if they did not sell she would not be out anything except possibly a little bit of her ego. The greatest part is, they sold quicker than she could have imagined!

A year later, that is now her MAIN source of income. She has more time available, more time with her girls, and she does not have to have two jobs just to get by. "I tend to look at things differently now," Marie told me, "I look at things in a more possible light and I approach things in a more upbeat manner. I see that there are opportunities out there if we would only allow ourselves to see them." Changing her consciousness about this subject has certainly benefited her!

After you start to be more mindful about the health of your thoughts, and make the negative mind chatter dissipate, you will start to notice how much better you feel and notice how much more compassionate you are. It is amazing how things can change for the better in your life. Just think of the more improved version of yourself that you can become!

Now that you have an understanding of how thoughts of yourself and others can affect you, including stopping your negative mind chatter and replacing it with good feeling thoughts, we can move on to dealing with stress. It will be shown how balance and flow are important, and practicing centering thoughts along with breath work is crucial. You will also discover how stress release is obtained through non-resistance.

Thoughts create things, so why not be more conscious in creating your future?

BALANCE AND FLOW

---

*"Just as your car runs more smoothly
and requires less energy to go faster and farther
when the wheels are in perfect alignment,
you perform better when your thoughts,
feelings, emotions, goals, and values are in balance."*

- Brian Tracy

Stress causes such havoc with your body. When you learn the art of balancing your values, you can obtain a lovely flow in life. I am not going to kid you. Some days are better than others for me. But I will also tell you, when I am in this zone it feels so good and so right. Complete zen. What is there not to love about that? I compare it to surfing on a wave. When it is right, it feels so great to have the wind whipping your hair, the rush of the joy of the experience. You know you have got it! It feels great. Sometimes you fall off, but you can get back on. Sometimes the experience lasts longer than other times. Yes, this takes some effort, but the rewards are phenomenal.

Balance is such an important piece of life. There are so many outside diversions in our life on a daily basis. If you have the knowledge or practices to help you maintain your balance, you can reach into that handy "tool box" of yours and implement accordingly to make your life as smooth sailing as possible.

When stress attacks you: Take a deep breath (or several as needed). Breathe into your belly. Now set this first thought before the natural doom and gloom may set in: "All is well" because ultimately all IS well. You are still alive and kicking; you have so much to be thankful for. This puts things into perspective. Next thoughts: "Is this really worth worrying about, and if so, to what level of worry?" I am actually not a fan of the word worry, because it implies the state of fretting over a problem. And if you are fretting, you are not in solving mode. It is actually quite the opposite. To solve a problem, your mind has to be in a totally different state. There are some times where we get ourselves worked up over things, that in the whole scheme of things, do not really matter. Traffic is a perfect example of this. Yelling at other drivers, or the traffic lights does not actually help; it can actually lead to multiple health problems, besides the possible random angry gun-slinging motorist next to you.

So take a deep breath, know that you will get to where you are headed in divine time, and go with the flow. You are not only going to live a more harmonic life, you will affect those around you with your positive energy!

As for traffic (which this coincided with so many other things in my life), I started realizing I did not need to pass everyone on the road and rush to where I was going. I started to be more aware of my surroundings, noticing the coolest little things that I was aware most others were missing. More and more the traffic lights I came to were green or turned green as I got to them. It was in an eerie but good kind of way. When I cease resisting things of this nature in my life and began to just 'allow,' things start coming so much easier to me! Even now, if things start to 'bind up,' I remind myself to go with the flow of life, and things immediately get easier and easier! It is amazing to see how I was in such a resisting mode for quite some time. Are you letting things flow in your life?

Arlene was the workaholic type of person that was sick all the time. If there was a flu-like symptom going around, she was sure to get it. She stressed about being sick all the time. There were never enough hours in a day, especially if she had to take time off because she was sick. This literally would drain her energy to think of it. She was complaining to one of her co-workers about it one day when they replied back to her, "Do you work to live, Arlene, or live to work?" That question stopped her in her tracks. She went home that night and pondered the way she had been living and dealing with her stresses. She was not happy. She knew she had to make a change. There was a local group that met weekly on how to deal with stress in life. She started going and incorporated the methods of breath work and relaxation throughout the day. She learned to take time to have fun and balance her work and play daily. She slowed her pace down, instead of being the whirlwind in her workplace, and was able to make deliberate, impactful, quality contributions daily. Her sick days used now are next to none and she feels better about her quality of life. She is super happy she made these changes to her life before her health had gotten any worse.

Another example is shown through my friend Johanna. When Johanna thought about having a baby with her husband, Jeremy, her mind would start to race. *What if the baby was born with a learning disability? What if her insurance did not cover all of the medical expenses? What if she could not get decent childcare, making it a challenge to go back to work? What if the house they had was too small for the three of them?*

These were just a tip of the iceberg. They had been trying to get pregnant for a while, without any results. Jeremy was raised with a laid back family, who had passed onto him the ways of more stress-less living. After one day of hearing her kick into high gear with a bunch of negative 'what if's', he had had enough. "Johanna, listen to yourself! Take a deep breath! You have not come up for air since you started on this rampage! Every scenario you just laid out was negative. Could you please start to think: "How great it is going to be to have a happy healthy baby? Won't it be great to go back to work and know that our child has a great daycare provider? Could you please try to not worry about every possible thing that could go wrong and think what could go right?"

After taking a few deep breaths and letting what Jeremy said sink in and marinate, she felt a weight come off of her shoulders. She had not realized what she had sounded like. He continued in a softer tone, "No matter what happens, we will love our baby, and ultimately that is all that matters in my eyes. We can not foresee every possible thing that may come up, and I do not want to, because that is the joy of life...Life's little surprises." She vowed from that moment on to start to look at things from that point of view and asked for his assistance if she started down that negative path. He willingly said yes and before the year came to an end, they found out they were going to be parents!

Going with the flow and maintaining your balance can provide you more of a stressless life. When you incorporate the simplest of breath work and centering thoughts like, "All is well," and not worry about things that are out of your control, you can release a lot of unneeded stress baggage. Letting that go will make room for more good things in your life, and I have a feeling you would not mind that at all!

Now you know why balance and flow is important, and how practicing centering thoughts along with breath work is crucial in stress release, and how *that* in turn is obtained through non-resistance. Now we will tie in self-love/care and how being authentic makes you flourish in life. People will want to know what your secret is when they see you radiate wherever you go!

In the end, look back on everything you have done in your life and see the lessons you have learned and the experiences you have had. If you knew then, what you know now, do you not think the perfect phrase to get you through any of those not-so-wonderful experiences could be "All is well"? Why not use that from here on out?

IT'S ALL ABOUT YOU

"It's not your job to like me – it's mine."

- Byron Katie

When you take care of yourself and give self-love, you flourish! Compare this to a flower, if you do not water it, give it care, it withers away. You deserve to receive this from others, but it all starts with you giving it to yourself. Go get that massage, *guilt free*, because you deserve it! Start rewarding yourself for your accomplishments. Tell yourself you are proud of yourself for being YOU. Initially, this was a much harder task than I had thought it was going to be. It sounded so simple. When I performed an exercise out of the book, "May Cause Miracles" by Gabrielle Bernstein, I looked in the mirror and told myself "I love you" I broke down and cried and was wondering what the heck that was all about! It gets easier and it makes more sense as you practice self-love.

The other part of this is being authentic. Who is the real you? Think of your values and act in line with them. When making decisions, do you always put others first? Please remember that what you think, say, and do matters, and when you do this with integrity, there is no room for regret or shame. While consideration of others is thoughtful, be careful not to give your own power away to others. What you say matters and ultimately you do know what is best for you.

As for your diet, if you put nutrition-deprived items into your body, your body will act accordingly. Think about the quality of the food that you put into your body. It is like the time I put some bad fuel in my car; it would spit and sputter and not have the power I was used to it having. Same idea, really.

Along with this, anything consumed while having a negative feeling attached to it will cause it to have a negative effect on your body. Everybody knows of that person that can eat whatever they want and they do not gain a pound. Ask them about their relationship with food. I am sure it does not consist of a slice of carrot cake with a side of guilt.

Remember to keep a well-balanced diet. I feel that certain "not so good things," IN MODERATION are ok. If you savor each morsel of an actual portion size, instead of wolfing down an entire sleeve of cookies, you are going to feel better knowing you enjoyed it. The key: enjoyment without guilt or regret.

Right now is the most important time to start giving yourself the gentle care you would give a special guest in your home. When you do this, you will thrive in ways you had possibly never even thought of! Why wait?

Make the call to the doctor you have been wanting to get in with. Go to the chiropractor because your back is not going to 'fix itself'. Schedule a massage because you are worth it! What is something that is on your list of things to do for fun, that you have been putting off? No more excuses! The benefits of these seemingly simple things are astronomical. When I started to research this, I was blown away. When I started implementing these things, they totally lit me up. Life was getting really good the more I did it.

I remember my mom telling me as I was growing up, "Where there's a will, there's a way". I truly believe that if you set an intention to do something with a pure heart, you will succeed! You need to do things for yourself. Whether it is self-care or starting a business you have been yearning to do. And the best part, is that it normally is not as hard as you think it will be. Remember that, "Doubt kills more dreams than failure ever will". Trust me, I have mastered a lot of seemingly hard things in my life and kept that quote in the back of my head. I love to think of the people before me perhaps that have done a hurdle that I am looking upon. And if I am pioneering, I know I have the strength because of my strong past that I can go where no one has gone before! This changes a once questionable perception into an "I can" attitude. Have the confidence that you can do it just as good, if not better, and get to it! AND have fun while doing it!

When I figured out my Top Three Values, one of them was Health/Well-Being. Pondering this I had to laugh. For it being in the Top 3, I sure was not acting that way. But that is okay, because I was now more aware of it and I knew I could make necessary changes! I started to eat better and savor more, picked up fun exercises and tried yoga (which I had on the "wish list" to do), I started putting better information in my mind (cut out all of the negative news that I could!), started meditating (another thing on the "wish list"), started drinking more water, and actually scheduled important doctor's appointments with doctors I really believed in and who would take the time for me. I had put a lot of these things off, because at the time, I had just "retired early" from my great paying job that had all of the benefits. So I did not have any health insurance. I decided I would stop using that as an excuse and bit the bullet and made my appointments anyway.

It worked out because what I had been paying in deductions I put aside monthly to pay for my visits, so it was working out nicely.

Plus, my health was getting better and better, so there was less of a need for prescriptions and extra appointments and so on. It was interesting to see all of the things I had put off for so long. And for what? So I could keep complaining about them? That was the bottom line.

I was spending more on groceries, because I was eating better quality items, but it is totally worth every penny in the long run. I do believe it has all worked out to my benefit in a multitude of ways! Yes, this example may not work for everyone. I do know that my change in perception and attitude has been a significant factor in this! Where in your life do you think you could make subtle changes that would make positive effects? Sometimes it is not so obvious.

Tori is the prime example of an over-giver. She always gave to others, would make time for others, but always shortchanged herself. She was having severe back pain and kept pawning it off. "It will work itself out," she would tell herself and others as they saw her wince as she was insisting on taking the heavy end of her friends couch to move it into a new apartment. "I just need to stretch it out," she would say as an excuse. On top of that, she was starting to break out in some sort of 'adult acne' she decided to call it.

Well, one day, her back went out and she could not go to work. She went to the doctor and they said she was going to have to take some time off from work and get an MRI. After she got the results back from the MRI, it revealed she had a herniated disc and her doctor said his recommendation was surgery. She asked if there were any other ways to help this situation besides surgery, like physical therapy. He said it may help, but it would not make the herniated disc go away. She decided to take the time and do the PT and see how that went. She was able to do some exercising, which she had not made time to do for herself and realized the difference that was beginning to make.

Slowly she was making progress, until she was able to go back to work full-time. Only then did she realize how important it was for her to take the time to strengthen her core and to exercise, not only because it was improving her back, but overall she was feeling better. She had also started making time for regular massages, which were making her feel on top of her game as well. While at the place she was receiving massages, she saw they had a special on facials for a limited time. She decided she would try it and got a facial the same day. It made her skin feel luxurious and she saw an improvement in her skin tone immediately. She got some tips from the provider on skincare, and she made the investment to start taking better care of her skin. The more time she was taking for herself, the better she was doing.

In this whole experience, she began to realize, the need for her to start to put herself first. Her back pain is no longer, now that she knows she has to keep up on her core exercises, and she has radiant skin, because she gives it the nourishment it needs.

Even if you feel that you do sufficient self-love/care maintenance, I dare you to amp it up and see what happens. Stick to respecting the things that you want to do, even if that means making boundaries with other people. Stay in your authentic self. I have a good feeling that you will start to feel more confident, have a certain radiance about you, and people will start to wonder what you have been doing because they will want some of that! Ultimately, if you remember you deserve it, you will flourish!

Is it not great to know that you have learned more about self-love/care and how being authentic makes you flourish in life, and having people wanting to know what your secret is when they see your radiance wherever you go! This idea will help you understand the next idea of meditation and the benefits of quieting your mind. This is a great self-care item that gives you great health benefits, and also releases residual stress and helps to make you feel better overall.

When you nourish yourself, your authentic self, you will radiate like a flower that is freshly blossomed among the drab weeds.

MEDITATE

"Meditation is not just for relaxation;
its primary purpose is to develop the capacity
to respond skillfully and gracefully
to life's difficulties as well as its joys."

- Shyalpa Tenzin Rinpoche

The health benefits alone from meditating are what I consider miraculous! Lowering stress levels and ultimately causing healthier blood pressure were good enough reasons for me to encourage everyone to take up meditating. For me personally, activating the creative flow was super awesome. I could not really fathom it, how it all works, or why it does. So I dabbled in research just a little. But it got to the point where I just wanted to try it. And I now think, "Man, if I had been doing this all along...I would be so much farther in life!" But I was not really ready for it until the day I committed to doing it.

Starting it now will improve your life. I was a bit skeptical at first, but I am so glad I started the practice of it, like I am sure you will be too! A big challenge for me at first was finding the time. It is funny that when I first had that thought, this quote by St. Francis De Sales appeared somewhere throughout that day: "Half an hour's meditation each day is essential, except when you are busy. Then a full hour is needed."

Finding someone who already does the practice of it or can guide you is super beneficial. Start by trying five or ten minutes and working your way up. I also set a gentle sounding timer on my phone to let me know when it is time to stop, so my thoughts are not constantly on the clock. Of course there are a multitude of meditating tips online and FAQs to help assist you in this journey. That helped me tremendously. Trying to stop all thoughts was frustrating. The stuff that comes up when I have to sit quiet and still my mind can sometimes be quite comical. I meditate with my journal at my side and write things that come to me. This is highly recommended, as I came up with some amazing 'downloads' that seemed to come out of thin air. This is the hint for you to incorporate Chapter 1's thoughts of journaling into this system...

The great news is, you get better at it as you practice! Then, you look forward to it so much in your daily regimen that it is just like my cup of coffee in the morning...my day is not the same without it!

I love to meditate for twenty minutes in the morning to get my day started. I have learned, as I have gotten better in my practice, to set an intention in uncovering a solution to a question at the beginning of my meditation. Then I let it go completely. The things that come to me, brilliant ideas or images during meditation or throughout the day have increased tremendously since I have started this process.

When I start to feel overwhelmed and "realistically" it seems as if the last thing I should be doing is meditation, that is exactly what I go to do. The spinning in my mind quiets down and I am able to think clearer, and I ultimately make more progress than if I had not taken twenty minutes to do so. I remember trying to meditate when I was younger and thinking to "properly" do it, I had to sit with my legs crossed, which was extremely uncomfortable for me. So I thought to sit on a chair was to do it "wrong," and I did not want to do it "wrong", so I did not do it at all. Now I know that there is more than one way to do it and you cannot really do it "wrong". Phew! I also learned that there are different types of meditations, so you can find one that appeals to you and branch out and try different ones.

I have this friend, Raymond, who was the type of person that had a million things going on, and he never took a moment to sit down, because there was always something that had to be done. He would multitask so much that anybody from the outside could see that if he would just focus on one thing from start to finish, it would get done faster than starting five things and attempting to keep them all going at once, like a juggling act. He would get frazzled, overwhelmed, and irritated because things would fall apart. He knew he had to do something different.

One day, he passed by a book sale on the street and saw a book on meditation. He had always wanted to try it; the people that did it always seemed so calm and appeared to him they had their 'stuff' together. To him, they never seemed to get overwhelmed, or at least it looked like they knew how to deal with it accordingly if they ever did have a moment like that. He snatched up the book for $1 and was on his way. It sat on his end table for a couple of weeks before he was feeling completely overwhelmed one day. He knew he was ready now, more than ever. He was ready to try anything to feel better!

Reading through and learning the techniques, he started to practice it. He started little bits at a time, at first with his mind racing so much he figured he was the only person on earth that could 'fail' at this. But he was persistent. Once in a while, he would feel the moments of peace that he longed for. And after those moments, when he was done meditating, his mind was clearer and more organized. He realized that he had to cut back on the amount of things he was working on all at once, prioritize, and then start and finish one thing and move onto the next. It seemed that he was taking more 'breaks' now to meditate or rest, yet he was getting more done and doing less running in circles. He compares it to the tortoise and the hare story! And he now recommends meditation to anybody he sees that is living the lifestyle that he was not long ago.

When you use your patience and allow yourself to relax into meditation, you will most likely wonder what took you all this time to discover it for yourself! Putting all of the scientific facts aside of why it is good for you, you can just feel better by incorporating this into your lifestyle. Who does not want to feel better?

Now you know about meditation and the benefits of quieting your mind. You know that there are great health benefits, and that it also releases residual stress and helps to make you feel better overall. Now we can move into the benefits of exercise, including the benefits of yoga, getting blood flowing, and chakra clearing. You will see why it is important to do what you are drawn to.

I could go on all day about what the benefits of meditation are for myself, but at the end of the day, when you try it and stick with it, you will get the results that *you* want, and that is what is most important.

EXERCISE

"Keeping your body healthy is an expression of gratitude to the whole cosmos – the trees, the clouds, everything."
- Thich Nhat Hahn

Getting your blood flowing triggers endorphins. This is not only your body's natural happy drug, it boosts your metabolism, and your thinking process too! Sounds like an easy "cure-all" to me! Improving your lifestyle by fun exercise is the greatest way to get started. FUN exercise. Basically just find the thing or things that you enjoy doing that gets your blood pumping. I am not the type that likes to do a gym routine at all. I prefer my own house and nature and I love variety! So get out there and start to explore all of the different options! Yes, some may be better choices than others, but ultimately you have to want to do them, not feel like you have to do them.

Another way of keeping your body healthy is by chakra clearing. Clearing the chakras is more of a new age kind of way of balancing and raising your energy. Yes, it works.

If you are not familiar, let me give you a super quick explanation of your chakras. Your body has seven chakras in which energy flows through. Each chakra represents different energy and is also represented with its own color. They are centered in the body as follows:

1st Chakra
Root
Red

The base of your spine, representing being grounded, emotionally representing survival issues.

2nd Chakra
Sacral
Orange

The lower abdomen, representing our connection with others and experiences, issues of abundance, sexuality, well-being, as well as pleasure.

3rd Chakra
Solar Plexus
Yellow

The upper abdomen, representing our personal power, issues of confidence and control, self-esteem.

4th Chakra
Heart
Green

The heart area, represents one's ability to love, issues of inner peace, love and happiness.

5th Chakra Throat *Blue*	The throat area, represents the way we communicate, issues of self-expression of one's feelings and speaking your truth.
6th Chakra Third Eye *Indigo*	Between your eyes on your forehead, represents seeing the big picture, issues with intuition, wisdom, decision-making, imagination.
7th Chakra Crown *Violet*	Top of the head, connection to spirituality, issues with pure bliss, spirituality and inner as well as outer beauty.

In order to stay healthy and balanced, it is important to keep these areas unblocked. While there are many techniques to help assist you in chakra clearing, certain exercises help with the physical part of it. Yoga is one of the many ways I like to assist in keeping my chakras in balance.

Thinking about *having to* workout drained the energy right out of me. It was not until I realized that I had to change my perception of exercising that I shifted my thoughts to, "I am going to jump on the trampoline because it is fun" rather than focusing on the fact that jumping on a trampoline for ten minutes has equivalent benefits to running just over thirty minutes. I also love to walk in nature for multiple reasons, but the added benefit is the exercise. See where I am headed in this thought process? It becomes effortless really; it is all in how you look at it. Being fit and healthy becomes a lifestyle that is natural, rather than a chore that you have to do every day.

Laura was the type of person that did not like to go to the gym and be seen in public doing any type of exercise, because she was self-conscious of her body and her weight. She was not athletic and compared her flexibility to a steel rod - it was not happening. She had always thought that yoga would be fun to try, but shuddered at the thought of taking a class and being surrounded by people doing near impossible pretzel-like moves, while she could not even touch her toes. But she was still interested in trying it out.

She saw in her local department store, in the workout aisle, a "Yoga For Beginners" DVD. It sounded like it was written especially for her. You could do it in the privacy of your own home, you could be the most non-flexible person on the planet, and it gave great directions and tips on doing it right. It also explained how each pose was affiliated with clearing these things called chakras that she had never heard of. She was so excited that she bought a yoga mat as well and could not wait to try it out when she got home. She liked the video, some poses were easier than others, and she felt herself getting better at it as time went on.

To her surprise, yoga had a lot to do with breathing. She always felt energized afterwards and felt better about her body. Her body was starting to get leaner and she decided to reward herself with buying a new outfit or two. She also decided to get outside and start walking more and even tried running for a short ways, gradually building up her distances. She looked at that as she had her yoga, start small and build on it. Now she looks for fun, new things to try that appeal to her. She knows if she is having fun doing it, she will stick with it.

I am sure you already have something in your mind that you would like to do, even if it does not meet burning the "1000 calories an hour" standards of what the ego says you 'should' be doing. I feel it does not matter, because if you went that route, you would psyche yourself out to not even attempt that anyway or complain about it and quit after a month of doing it. We have all done that. When you pick that thing that you are drawn to that makes you want to do it, it makes it ...dare I say it...EASY and FUN! So go and get started and see where it takes you! And it is okay to change things up, just do *something*!

It feels good to now know more about the benefits of exercise, including the benefits of yoga, getting blood flowing, and chakra clearing. It is also great to now understand why it is important to do what you are drawn to. This easily ties into the next chapter, since so many activities we like to do are outside. Next you will see more about how nature can put things into perspective, energize you, clear your mind, balance and ground you to melt stress away.

In the end, it is all about triggering your body's endorphins which is not only your body's natural happy drug, it boosts your metabolism, *and* your thinking process too!

NATURE

"Look deep into nature, and then you
will understand everything better."
- Albert Einstein

Getting out in nature helps us reconnect with our source. It puts things in perspective. It can lessen stress levels in an instant. The feeling of freedom is easy to recapture. It can ground you when you are feeling overwhelmed.

This is an easy, free and natural way of assisting you in getting balanced.

Regardless of what is going on; if you are having a good day, a stressful one, feeling stuck, or having a sluggish moment, take time and go outside and connect with nature. Nature puts things into perspective. Its beauty, in so very many ways can enhance your life, when you choose to look at it and truly see it. It is a reminder that the simplest things are worth taking the time to appreciate. If having a stuck moment, going outside can help clear the air in your mind, much like a meditation. When you stop thinking about a problem while outside, it can re-boot your mental process so you can see things in a different way altogether, shedding new light on a situation. So go take a walk or just sit and listen, look around and just notice things.

Being raised surrounded by nature and learning to appreciate it at a young age helped me so much throughout my life. With constantly going for walks, even in the rugged weather the Northeast would bring, my family would still be out in nature each and every day. Being raised on a farm, there were chores that had to be done in the outdoors daily, but we were always encouraged to have the time to enjoy a walk to break away from the work part of it.

I remember my mom stopping mid step and having my sister, my cousin and I quiet down for a moment to listen to the birds or the peepers or stop and smell the ferns of the forest. We would giggle and think it was silly, but I can appreciate now what she was passing down. And it did stick with me. I love going for walks and stopping mid stride to appreciate the bald eagle that is flying directly over my head or the leaves I am kicking up as I walk through the woods. Nature has so much to teach us if we would just take the time to listen. I have been indulging in this more and more recently and I am so amazed at the things that can be easily overlooked.

Anne loves her corporate job. She is good at what she does and makes everybody else's job around her easier by her brilliant brainstorming skills. One day, she was stumped on what seemed to be something that should be an easy fix. The people around her wanted to take the easy way out and solve the problem by doing it the way they had always done it. It was gnawing at her, because she knew she could think of a better way, it just was not coming to her.

She decided for lunch to just take her sandwich outside and get out in the sun that was very inviting that day. She put her pen down and decided not to think about this problem that she needed the answer to until after she got back. So while eating lunch, she sat by the river and just took a moment to unwind. She watched the fish jump in the water, the ducks all swimming in a row and the geese on the bank with their babies. The birds were chirping and fluttering about and a dragonfly curiously circled her and then flew off. She marveled in the way all of nature was getting along, and seemed to work together in a sense.

It was then time to go back inside and on her way back to her desk she almost broke into a run. It hit her, "I have an idea to solve our problem! It involves working individually, yet together as a whole, just as all of nature was doing outside!" By the end of the day she was presenting her idea to her boss and her peers, and she was congratulated with thinking of yet another brilliant strategy for the company. Now she goes outside for her morning and afternoon breaks, because that time outside brings her the clarity she needs. It also seems to recalibrate her balance to be the best that she can be.

When you make sure to get out into nature every day, at least once a day, you can feel a better sense of peace. Putting things into perspective can help assist you in life's daily encounters. You may even realize that for you, you inexplicably feel more balanced. I always encourage that if it feels good to you, then do it!

It is so great to know more about how nature can put things into perspective, energize you, clear your mind, balance and ground you to melt stress away. In the next chapter, we will uncover the importance of gratitude and how when we give it, we can receive more good things in our life! You will also learn how it is the quickest way to get you out of a not so good feeling thought!

Nature - get out in it and receive all of the benefits it has to offer you!

GRATITUDE IS THE ATTITUDE

"Gratitude opens the door to... the power,

the wisdom, the creativity of the universe.

You open the door through gratitude."

- Deepak Chopra

When you give gratitude and feel the appreciation for what is, more of it will be drawn to you. It is as simple as that. It is the Law of Attraction in motion. I am pretty sure you are wanting more good things in your life. Ultimately, you want to do it because it makes you feel good! Remember, life is meant to be enjoyed!

Notice the way you feel when you experience gratitude, warm and fuzzy inside, like a million bucks. Now take it one step further. If you are giving gratitude to someone for something they did, think about how they feel when you shower them with it, pretty sweet. Go even farther and think about somebody else witnessing you giving another person that thanks. Catch my drift? It is a snowball effect. This is a great train to be on, right? If you are having a rough day or moment, the easiest way to turn it around is to look for something you are grateful for.

I remember a time when I really had to reach, but the greatest part is that I never went that "low" again! Seriously! I started with a gratitude journal. I looked around and decided I was thankful for my indoor plumbing. (Yes, I was at a very low point when I was starting with that thought!) I really had to dig deep at that point and see I was very blessed to be where I was in my life, all things considered. I was living a life of luxury compared to 80% of the rest of the world. My thoughts of gratitude began to ascend more and more, and in doing so I progressively came out of such a slump; it is amazing to see how far I have come. You will have those moments where you are naturally on top of the world and everything goes right! Those are the moments I am most grateful for, and I will admit, they are coming more and more frequently. One of my favorite mantras: "Thank you, Thank you, Thank you!" It automatically makes me smile!

Thomas was having a low point in his life. He had what in his mind was a crappy job, he was getting frustrated with his home and he felt like he did not have a lot of good in his life. One day while surfing the internet, he came across a site that encouraged people to write what they were grateful for in their life. He read through the ones that were posted there and decided he could find something he could write. He was touched by the things that other people had written and realized in looking around he actually had a lot to be thankful for.

After writing he was thankful for his warm home that he could call his own, he decided to write on a piece of paper 50 things he was grateful for. He was surprised his hand could barely keep up with his thoughts. After looking at the list of everything he wrote, he felt really good inside. He decided that every single day for the rest of the year he would write down ten things that he was grateful for. He was a little worried that he would run out of things, but figured he would cross that bridge when he got there. To make it easier he kept a journal on his nightstand, so in the morning, he would write down five things and at the end of the day he would write another five.

He started to notice something wonderfully strange start to happen. More good things started to come into his life. He started to improve his home, it felt more welcoming and he was loving it more. He started focusing on the good aspects of his job and his workdays were going faster. His job was not dragging him down anymore, like it had been. He started seeing a woman he had often admired at the laundromat he frequented. She said she had never really noticed him until recently, and she struck up a conversation over the drying cycle. He has not had a problem coming up with his daily ten things and has already surpassed his year-long goal of doing it!

In finding things to be grateful for, it is only natural to see more of the good things in your life to be grateful for. As this snowballs, you will *attract* even more things to be grateful for. It is a wonderful cycle, really. This will encourage you to have better and better thoughts more of the time. Just start by thinking of the things that YOU are grateful for and see where this takes you.

Now you have uncovered the importance of gratitude and have also learned how it is the quickest thing to get you out of a not so good feeling thought.

Is it not amazing to know the synergy that gratitude can carry and how it is such an easy thing to do? You can access these thoughts at any time! This is an amazing tool in your toolbox of manifesting things that you want! Feel the power!

ON YOUR WAY

"All souls have the
capacity to be great souls"
- Gary Zukav

Congratulations! You are awesome! Way to go on finishing this life changing book and taking on the challenge to implement these great strategies in your life! If you have been doing the practices as you have been going along, I can only imagine the great things that have been happening for you already! Keep up the great work!

As you can see, you can journal about every section in this book. Use each chapter as a guide to journal about.

Keep checking in with yourself to feel how you are doing and try to recognize what you need. Revisit any chapters if needed and start to do little things in your life that keep you inspired to be the person that you want to be.

As I was almost finished writing this book, I had an unusually bad day. I was in a total funk, not like me at all. I felt like I was wandering around and I could not get out of my own tracks. Ever have one of those days? I felt like I was in no shape to give the world any guidance that day, so I did not want to write. I finally motivated myself to read what I had written already. I actually laughed at loud. It was like I had forgotten everything that I had written on paper. As if I had forgotten my super strategies that work! Immediately, I started incorporating them. I began to feel so much better. This is actually quite embarrassing for me to admit. But I wanted to show you how it can be easy to get off-track, and it can be just as easy to get back on. Now, if I feel myself 'going there', I make quick reference back to my book and it really sets me straight. True story!

Make sure to use the strategies you have learned daily, and you will continue to see amazing results! Notice how you feel when you receive the rewarding results from implementing each chapter's strategies. This will be incentive to keep up what you have been working on!

When you implement the ways discussed in the book and as you get more comfortable, if you feel inspired, go ahead and explore and develop your favorite techniques. Just start with what I have given you and branch out in whatever ways are pulling you!

My life changed subtly at times and more drastic at other times. It was fun to keep track by writing it down. I love looking back at things that I do not remember as vividly until I read about them and recall. It is nice to keep 'score' of the good things in my evidence journal because it has given momentum to more of those good things to come into my life. Even as I was writing this book, amazing things were happening, and I believe it is because I have been in such a great place while I was writing it! It is beyond rewarding! I love to talk about it and encourage others to get to a better feeling place that they want to be! And to think it all started for me by just knowing I had to make a choice to take a chance in doing something different from what I had been doing, in order for my life to change for the better!

I sense what you and everybody is looking for. While a million dollars may or may not be on your list of things you wish to create, I have a feeling when you decided on your Core Values, it was not in your top three. I have a feeling it was something of more substance than material things. Yes, while we all agree those things are nice, they ultimately mean nothing if you do not have the time to enjoy them or if you have no loved ones to share the joy with. I recognize that it is not the money I desire, but the freedom it brings! I can visualize you feeling that harmony that you desire. I can see you having more joy and appreciation of the little and the big things in life. I can see you receiving and experiencing the things that you want to be, do, and have. I believe you are going to have a renewed sense of living, like looking at life in a whole different way. Your energy will be uplifted all by you and your daily actions.

It means so much to me that I can share this great knowledge with you. I appreciate you taking the time for YOU and learning these great ways to help you create your more fulfilling life. It is truly a gift to me to know that you get at least one 'aha' moment in implementing any of these strategies.

Remember, you get out of it what you put into it. This is your life to create however you want and you have the power to do it! Do it now, or forever wish you had....

FREQUENTLY ASKED QUESTIONS

Q: What if I don't feel like journaling?

A: Just try it! Please understand that writing things down can show intention, assist in giving clarity, help you move through things and also manifest things along the way. Just try doing it a little bit every day. If you want different things in your life, you have to start doing things differently, and this is one of the simple things that can help you improve tremendously.

Q: Why is it so important to get outside every day at least once a day?

A: Getting out in nature helps us reconnect to our source. It puts things in perspective. It can lessen stress levels in an instant. The feeling of freedom is easy to recapture. It can ground you when you are feeling overwhelmed. It can energize you if you are having a 'blah' moment as well!

Q: If I already know what is important to me, do I still have to go through the Core Value exercise?

A: Yes. Keep in mind that mine were not what I initially would have thought. Interesting, right? That is why it is so important to do this exercise! When I focused on my core values, I considered these more in my daily decision-making and I actually began to make wiser decisions! It seems like such a simple thing, like we should just "know", but it is amazing to see the daily moves that we make mindlessly. Then you can see if you have been making decisions in your life, inline with your core values and perhaps where you need to make some much needed changes!

Q: Will uncovering my self-limiting beliefs really make a difference in my life?

A: Since 90% of your brain capabilities are run with subconscious thoughts, this definitely affects your decision process. The other 10% is the conscious brain. The majority of these thoughts were actually formed at a very young age, and you probably do not realize what power they have. You can take control of more of your thoughts and use them in a good way. You can realize the things that are holding you back that you do not consciously realize and become the best person that you can be. It could make a huge difference really.

Q: Why are thoughts about myself and others important?

A: When one has not-so-nice mind chatter, it acts as a poison residing in your own self. As for putting yourself down, you can unknowingly stop yourself from ascending in life. You will start to notice how much better you feel and notice how much more compassionate you are when you become more conscious of your thoughts and manage them accordingly. What is not to like about a more improved version of you?

Q: What are your favorite stress management techniques?

A: I take a deep breath (or several as needed) into the belly. I use my mantra, "All is Well". This puts things into perspective. Then I think, "Is this really worth worrying about, and if so, to what level of worry?" To solve a problem, I know my mind has to be in a totally different state and I act accordingly. This helps in centering my thoughts and also with any stressful situation that comes up.

Q: What if I feel like I do sufficient self-love/care things for myself?

A: Amp it up and see what happens. Know you are worth it and you deserve it! Everybody does. Stick to respecting the things that you want to do, even if that means making boundaries with other people. Stay in your authentic self. People will start to wonder what you have been doing because they will want some of that!

Q: What if I try meditating and I mess it up?

A: First off, be patient with yourself. Finding someone who already does the practice of it or can guide you is super beneficial. Start by trying five or ten minutes and working your way up. It can be challenging at first, but there are different types of meditation and if you explore and try different ways, you will find the best ones for you. It does not happen all at once. You will start to recognize what a gap between thoughts is and figure out what works for you in achieving it. Stick with it. I have a feeling you will be super happy you did!

Q: I want to exercise, but the things that 'normal' people do, like go to the gym, do not appeal to me at all. Do you have any suggestions?

A: Just find something that you are drawn to that sounds fun, it does not have to be a proven all-time best fat-burning activity. If you are drawn to walking, swimming, trampoline time with the kids, do that. The important thing is that you are getting your endorphins activated. This not only is your body's natural happy drug, it boosts your metabolism, and your thinking process too!

Q: Is it just as important to give gratitude to the big things in my life as the small things?

A: YES! I love to take the time to give appreciation for the big things AND the small things, because ultimately I do appreciate them and I would like more of all of those great things in my life. It is the Law of Attraction in motion. When you give gratitude and feel the appreciation for what is, more of it will be drawn to you. Simple as that. And easy to boot!

Q: The idea of tapping seemed a little confusing to me. What can I do to understand it better?

A: Simply visit my website at www.SallyScofield.com/EFT to watch a training video I created just for you. You can watch how I perform the tapping movements and how I sync up the statements with the tapping. This will help you see how to do it for yourself. You can also follow along with me and benefit from it that way, too.

FINAL THOUGHTS

I realize that you reached for this book because you wanted something to change. Notice how when you intend for things to change for the better and keep that intention in your mind, they really do go in that direction. I was in that place, not all that long ago, and I am so happy to say I have created the life that I want and it is getting better and better every day in every way. Keep your chin up with a positive attitude and you *will* go far! I am so excited to see where you go!

No matter what life will seem to throw at you, there is always some sort of learning lesson and a positive spin you can put on it. It is all in how you decide to perceive it. You can be a victim or a creator in this life. I choose to create!

So everywhere you go, look for inspiration! Find inspiring quotes that help you go after your dreams. Do fun and silly things, like eat dessert before dinner. In the end, we are meant to have fun and LIVE our lives the way we want to. So do it now, do not wait for tomorrow! It is the perfect time to light up your life!

If you have any questions about this book, I would love to answer them!

Email me at info@SallyScofield.com.

I want to hear of your success stories! I love to hear of all of the great ways that the people that I have come into contact with have created the life that they want. Isn't it great when you hear an amazing story and how it inspires you and makes you feel good inside? It is my thrill and joy when I hear great things like this, so please share them with me anytime you want! Email me at info@SallyScofield.com and do not forget to visit my website at www.SallyScofield.com for more valuable insights on how to *Light Up Your Soul*.

ABOUT THE AUTHOR

Sally Scofield is naturally drawn to serving others in a uniquely helpful way. She has taken on the other side of the meaning "lightworker" since moving on from being a lineman at a large electric company in Upstate New York. She lights up a room with her presence and energy, emitting positive vibes wherever she goes. She is passionate about sharing her favorite manifesting techniques as part of the workshops she teaches locally. Sally also loves to help people uncover their life's purpose through the proven, scientific based system of Hand Analysis. She happily resides in her beautiful, peaceful home in Delhi, NY, with her significant other, Mike and their dog, Bud. She is an avid nature woman, spending as much time outdoors as possible. She loves working with Icelandic Horses when she is not raising the consciousness of others or saving the world by lighting up one soul at a time.

FREE DOWNLOAD

Tune in real quick and answer the following questions honestly:

- Do you wish you could discover a way to *Light Up Your Soul* every day in every way?

- Did you read my book and love all the ideas in but have no idea how you'll remember to implement them on a daily basis?

- Will you want to have an awesome tool that you can print out and use anywhere you want?

If you answered YES to any of the questions above, then be sure to download my free *Light Up Your Soul* Daily Checklist Poster!

Feel free to print out as many copies as you need. Post them on your wall, your desk, your mirror, or anywhere else in your home or office to serve as a daily reminder for you to implement my *10 Powerful Ways to Create a More Fulfilling Life.*

CLAIM YOUR FREE DOWNLOAD AT

www.SallyScofield.com

www.ingramcontent.com/pod-product-compliance
Lightning Source LLC
Chambersburg PA
CBHW021345090426
42742CB00008B/751